You are a Child of the King

You are a Child of the King

and He has an inheritance for you!

Keith Trumbo

ISBN 13: 9781693844805

Dedication

I would like to dedicate this book to my dad, Floyd D. Trumbo, who died in December of 2018. I would also like to thank Maurice and Nancy Franks, Gwen Simmons with Word Watch Editing, my wonderful, patient and beautiful wife Ann, and my son Taylor whose imagination and compassion for others inspire me.

YouAreAChildoftheKing.com

Table of Contents

Introduction

YOU ARE A CHILD OF THE KING

Do you live like a prince or princess with chauffeured limos, butlers, maids, and assistants to cater to your every need? Do you get invited to long parades where you ride in a horse-drawn carriage and wave to crowds lining the streets? How about your last meal? Was it served on expensive china and prepared by chefs with the best food money can buy? Do you enjoy wearing tailored suits or hand-made dresses from the finest cloth? Do you live the life of royalty?

Do you know that you are a child of the King, and you can live the life of royalty as a child of the King? That does not mean you will live in a mansion with butlers, servants, maids, and assistants of every kind. It does mean, however, that you are the focus of His love and affection. The King seeks to protect, heal, love, and teach you. As a child of the King, the King will bless you with every blessing He knows you need. He will protect you and provide peace beyond your understanding. He will uphold you and strengthen you, so fear will not direct your decisions. He delights in providing for you. He will shield you and be the solid rock foundation of your life. You will live with hope, unafraid of the unknown, and with an awesome future that He provides. Are you ready to discover how?

Part One

You Have an Inheritance

Y ou have a relative who has a very high position, the King of Kings, and you are His child. Born into His family, you are the focus of His attention. He knows and understands all the challenges you face each day. The King also knows all the inside information about your life. He knows your strengths and your weaknesses, He knows everything about you and still loves you as if you have never made a mistake or made a choice that does not honor Him. He knows all your secrets and still loves you more than any father could love his child.

The King offers you favor and love that exceeds the love and favor you received from your earthly parents. His love for you has no parallel. He accepts you no matter what your past includes because He is most interested in your future. He accepts people without prejudice toward the color of their skin or birthplace. He does not reject or treat people differently because of wealth, poverty, family, or political perspectives.

The King does not seek to condemn, He seeks to help with your disappointments and pain. He counts your tears and understands each challenge you face. He doesn't approach you with a you-don't-measure-up perspective. He welcomes you just as you are and seeks to listen to your concerns, hopes, and goals for the future.

The King knows that we can have deep injuries from people who claimed to represent Him, yet did not. In fact, it could be said that many people today have turned away from opportunities to embrace the King's love and grace to its fullest because of His followers who have not fully experienced the power of His love and grace.

The King accepts you, welcomes you, and embraces you, knowing that you have a problem. He accepts you because He knows He can solve your problem. Do you know about your problem that the King already understands about you? While you are a child of the King, you were born separated from Him. Separated from the King by the way you think. He has an unselfish, love-based approach and you were born with a self-centered approach. To solve your problem, the King can give you an inheritance that enables you to experience the power of His love and healing to the fullest, to fulfill your destiny of living as a child of the King.

The King can provide an inheritance that no one else can offer you, an inheritance that comes to you as a gift because your story goes back to Moses, Jacob, Isaac, Abraham, Noah, Adam and Eve. It is a story that defines your past and your future.

An inheritance becomes available to a person because someone died and included them in their last will and testament. Your inheritance comes to you because of the King's death on a cross. He gave all for you, He suffered, endured ridicule, shame, torture, and death at the hands of His creation because of His love and commitment to His creation. His death opens the door for you to inherit the power of His love in your life.

The inheritance He seeks to give you includes five special gifts, not because of good things you have done, not because you deserve it or have earned your inheritance, but because you were born His child, and He seeks to give you an opportunity to solve your problem.

The inheritance the King has for you includes:

The gift of assurance. You can start and end each day knowing that the King loves you and accepts you.

The gift of honesty. The ability to be honest as the King helps you understand the desires in your heart that can keep you from living a life of freedom.

The gift of enlightenment. Being enlightened means understanding the difference between the way the King thinks and the way you think, and why the King's way of thinking is better. Then, He can give you the strength to choose and follow His way of thinking.

The gift of apologizing when you fail. He can help you apologize for the mistakes you make. You can experience the healing of forgiveness that empowers the gift of apologizing.

The gift of discernment. The gift of discernment enables us to unmask the deceptions of the villain, the con artist, the scammer, the one who lies, cheats, and hates the King and seeks to make sure you never, ever receive your inheritance or experience the power of the King's love.

You can receive all these gifts each day. I will provide a more detailed explanation of these gifts later in the book. These five gifts He promises to give you will empower your life with clarity in a confusing world. You can be the one in your neighborhood who receives a powerful inheritance from the King of Kings so you can then experience the freedom, peace and healing He provides.

Your inheritance is more valuable than gold, silver or diamonds. However, you will not have to keep your inheritance in a safe. You will not need a key or a combination to access the gifts in your inheritance. You can receive valuable, real help each day from the King to guide you with the issues, challenges, and choices you make.

You do not need to change anything so you can qualify to receive your inheritance. You qualify right now. The King just asks one thing from you. To receive your inheritance you must meet the terms of the agreement the King designed. The terms are simple, yet vital. If you do not meet the terms of the agreement, you will not receive your inheritance.

As with most agreements, the agreement the King designed for us has two parts: His part and our part. His part of the agreement means He will provide us with the gifts in our inheritance each day for free, no charge, no cost. These gifts offer you real help to understand the unknown; to understand the difference between the way He thinks and the way we think, and why His way of thinking is better. His way of thinking is based on a foundation of love and unselfishness. Our natural way of thinking is based on self, what's good for me. The King offers us our inheritance for free because of His grace. In fact, we could never purchase the precious gifts He seeks to give us.

Our part of the agreement means that each day we ask the King to help us trust in Him. He responds with His grace by providing gifts that will enable us to have a real relationship with Him. As we ask for His help to trust in Him and even ask for His help to receive the five gifts in our inheritance, we can experience the power of His love to the fullest each day. By receiving the gifts in our inheritance, He can then help us understand His way of thinking with the choices we face in life. To ask for His help is a simple act, yet it is the greatest challenge we face in our lives.

When you enter into the agreement with the King to receive your inheritance, you are asking for His help to understand a new and fresh perspective. You're inviting the King to help you embrace a foundation of love for your choices. When you ask for and accept the gifts in your inheritance, the King can open His heart to you, explain to you, and reason with you, and dialogue with you about how to let His love illuminate the choices in your life. Asking to receive these five gifts each day enables you to have a real, personal relationship with your Creator. He designed you to have this kind of relationship with Him.

To embrace the agreement and receive your inheritance, you might begin to ask for His help with a prayer like this: "Dear King of Kings, I ask for Your help to trust in you. I ask for Your help to know how to receive Your help today. I am not sure what will happen or how you will respond to my request, yet I am willing to ask for your help today. I admit that I do not think as You do. I would like to know more about Your way of thinking."

I have found that the King knows the kind of help I need each day. He knows the kind of stealthy, hidden selfishness that can control my choices. He can give me the help I need to neutralize the plans of the villain for my life. I have discovered that I will get ensnared and entangled in one failure after another if I try to live a life that honors the King without His help. So, try it. You can ask for and receive the gifts in your inheritance that will empower you to have a personal relationship with the King. You can experience the power of His love to its fullest each day.

You won't ever graduate from needing to ask for His help to understand His way of thinking and to trust in Him. You won't grow to the point that you don't need His help. In fact, not realizing that you need His help, or being unwilling to ask for His help will cause you big trouble. If you do not ask for His help, you will use your own self-centered approach and either not follow the King or think you are following the King, yet you are really just following your own ideas.

The next section identifies some of the problems that come from a misunderstanding of faith which can keep people from living as children of the King. A clear understanding of faith opens the door to receive your inheritance and embrace a real relationship with the King.

Part Two

The King Wants a Real Relationship with You

You are a child of the King. Your story reveals that you're related to the King who gave His life for you. His death provides an inheritance that will empower you to have a real, personal relationship with the King.

To receive your inheritance, the King designed an agreement for you to embrace. The agreement has simple terms, yet presents a great challenge. The terms of the agreement say that you must receive your inheritance by faith. Unfortunately, many people do not have a healthy view of how faith works in their lives. Often people think of faith as just *believing in* the King.

With the King's help, faith becomes more than mere belief in the King, more than an acknowledgment of His existence, more than an acknowledgment of His death on the cross and resurrection. A simple acknowledgment of the facts in the King's life does not equal faith. Faith includes a knowledge of the events in the King's life, yet faith involves much more than merely believing He existed.

Some Christians refer to themselves as believers, setting themselves in opposition to others who do not believe. Then, as the thinking goes, the King rewards their belief and they receive blessings and material wealth from the King. However, honestly, that turns faith into something we do to earn the King's favor, doesn't it? Faith has more substance, more value than to just be a way to win favor with the King so He will do things for us.

Faith doesn't work like a currency to get what we want from the King. If you have enough faith, the thought goes, then you can get what you want from the King. If things are not working out well for you (the way *you* think things should go), then you do not have enough faith. In the middle of a challenge or crisis, has someone ever told you to just have faith?

Sometimes people compare faith to muscles in the body. The more we exercise our faith, the stronger we grow. Yet, with faith, the stronger we get, the more dependent (not independent) we become upon the King. Therefore, thinking that we can build our faith stronger and stronger, like a bodybuilder, so we can lift more weight for the King does not represent an accurate comparison.

People can also fall into the trap of looking at faith as obedience, thinking, *Whatever the King says, I will do.* That does not work. We should not mistake self-motivation or self-discipline for faith. Faith does not develop or empower a strong will. Faith does not mean we must embrace a stubborn, unyielding I-will-get-my-own-way form of obedience born from our own sense of duty.

Faith is our response to believing that we were born with a problem that only the King can help us solve. We understand that we have a different way of thinking than the King. With the challenge of a dominant self-interest we all possess, we can't understand or choose His way of thinking without His help. He is our Savior, meaning He is the One who "saves" us. We cannot "save" ourselves. To enter into the agreement which leads to a real relationship with the

King requires that we first believe that we need His help to trust in Him.

The King bases His way of thinking on a foundation of pure love, which is foreign to our way of thinking. Without His help, His way of thinking will be unknown to us. We need His help to both understand and choose His way of thinking. Faith becomes real when we know that we must have His help to trust in Him when things do not work out the way we want, and when they do work out the way we want. Faith leads us to live each day with a commitment to ask for His help to understand how to apply His love to the issues, challenges and situations we face.

Most often people think of faith in terms of results. If I have enough faith, then my expectations will be met. Yet that way of thinking leads to discouragement and ruin. Faith leads us to ask for the King's *help* with our choices and leave the *results* to Him. Therefore, if someone donated one hundred dollars to a church with the expectation that the King would somehow bless them with one thousand dollars in return, that represents a false expectation, a false faith. If we believe that with enough faith the King must heal our cancer, find us a better job, pay our credit card debt, or keep us from any tragedy, then we have a false faith.

When we believe that faith is something in us that makes the King act in a specific way, we have a false faith and can easily become disappointed or confused. When we expect or even demand a specific outcome from the King, this represents presumption. Real faith means we know we need His help to trust in Him, we believe that He will help us and as He helps us to trust in Him, we can leave the results to Him.

Have you been asking for His help to understand His way of thinking? Then, in His way and in His time He can help you with the issues, situations, and challenges you face whether they be cancer, financial troubles, finding the right person to marry, a new job, or a mistake you have made.

When you comply with the agreement by living with faith, and thus understand the reality of our human condition, you will live by asking for His help to trust in Him so you can receive the gifts in your inheritance. The gifts He provides will enable you to have a real, honest, productive and vibrant relationship with Him. Our relationship with the King does not grow as we force ourselves to trust in Him. It develops as we receive the gifts He provides which enable us to trust in His way of thinking.

So let's say you take the agreement for a test drive and invite Him to help you. What can you expect? Will you turn into a religious fanatic over night? Will you need to give away all your money and possessions to the poor and live in a simple shack eating rice and beans? What should you expect? Would it be worth giving this a try? Keep reading the next section. It goes into more detail about the agreement the King designed for you and how you can take it for a test drive.

Part Three

The King's Agreement for Your Inheritance

You are a child of a King. A King who understands your feelings, emotions, trials, hopes, dreams and challenges better than you understand them yourself. If you do not agree with that statement, you will have a hard time asking for His help. However, if you are even willing to ask for His help to know why you need to ask for His help, then He can help you.

The King does not seek to force you to follow His ways, like a conquered army or robot. He seeks a dialogue with you, where you ask questions, and let Him help you be honest about your own desires and motives without holding anything back. In fact, the King designed the agreement to receive your inheritance in such a way as to require that you dialogue or reason with Him. It is more than just asking for Help, you need to know why you need help.

He does not want you to follow Him blindly, just following His commands like a robot. But in a personal way, where you share your fears, dreams, hopes, and challenges with your King who already understands the deepest fears and dreams in your heart. As you invite Him to help you open up about the true feelings (that He already knows all about) you can have clarity and begin to understand the difference between His way of thinking and your human way of thinking.

The King loves you, accepts you and has an awesome future for you. You are His child. When you choose to uphold your part of the agreement, you will experience a miracle just as real as someone being healed from cancer or a man born blind receiving his sight.

When you uphold your end of the agreement by asking for His help to trust in Him, then the gifts in your inheritance enable you to ask for His help continuously, as a daily, hourly routine. You can embrace the joyous routine of requesting His help. He can then touch your heart with a peace that is beyond your understanding. He can calm your mind with the power of His love and help you see challenges in a different light. He can help you understand the difference between good and evil, right and wrong. He can soothe the pain of the unfair injustices of the past, knowing He is the final righteous Judge for all.

The King knows that at times it can be hard for us to accept all five of the gifts in our inheritance. Our inheritance leads us to face ourselves and that we like to avoid. Yet the agreement stands, the agreement does not waver or vary, it is the same for everyone. Because we are born with a self-centered perspective, we must have His help to understand His way of thinking.

In our thinking, we can get offended when our expectations are not met. We can develop distorted ways of thinking because of the painful, unfair, unjust and mean ways others have treated us. From dysfunctional relationships to outright evil, our painful experiences lead us to build walls around our hearts and make us guard and sometimes not even be aware of our innermost feelings.

The King knows all about unfair, unjust and evil treatment you have endured. He can heal the most painful situations you have experienced. He can bring healing to your heart from any cruel experiences from the past. He can also release you from any guilt you carry around from choices you regret. The King will do all this as you believe that you need a Savior and thus seek to have faith in the King. He will help you understand the unknown, understand the difference between the way you think and the way He thinks. This will bring the healing of forgiveness you need each day.

The unfortunate experiences we've encountered in this life make it impossible to trust in the King without His help. To think that we can understand the King's way of thinking without His help means we do not acknowledge the powerful influence of the painful experiences in our past and the deeply ingrained, stealthy selfishness that influences us each day.

The King designed the agreement to enable you to spend eternity with Him in His heavenly Kingdom. This earth does not operate the way the King originally intended. We all face a villain who intruded on the plans of the King. Yet in His heavenly kingdom, everything does operate as He intends. Therefore, everyone who goes to heaven will welcome the King's way of thinking here on earth. That is not to say they must become perfect to qualify for heaven. However, they will agree with what the King has shown them and want to know more. So, if we do not learn from the King about His way of thinking here on earth, how could we suddenly agree with His way of doing things in heaven?

Part Four

The Gifts in Your Inheritance

You might be surprised to understand that it is possible for someone to claim to be a Christian for many years and not take advantage of the agreement the King designed. Therefore, that means they have not received their inheritance, yet tried to live as a Christian. Which means churches can have some mean people as members who claim to be children of the King, but live controlling, political, critical, gossip-filled lives without being aware of their hypocrisy. Ouch!

While some people ignore the agreement, we also need to understand that the agreement is not a one-time choice that covers every future decision we will make. The agreement represents a way of life. Each day and with each issue we face we can take joy in asking for the King's help to trust in Him.

As the King provides the five gifts in our inheritance, He provides the real help we need to solve our problem and overcome the villain. As we invite Him, He will help us understand the difference between His way of thinking and our way of thinking. Then, as we understand why His way of thinking is best, we can ask for His strength to follow His way. Yet, if we choose our way of thinking over His way, He will help us understand our mistake and why it was a mistake. Then we can admit our mistake to Him and anyone we have injured. So, in that way, even the mistakes we make become opportunities to learn more about the King and ourselves.

Here is a more detailed explanation of the five gifts in your inheritance that enable you to have a genuine, personal relationship with the King:

1. The Gift of Assurance
Assurance. What a precious and valuable gift! You can begin and end each day knowing that the King loves you and accepts you. You do not need to lose hope with the challenges you experience. The King went to extreme measures to give you an opportunity to get to know Him. He even counts your tears, and He understands your pain and grief. As you continue to ask for His help and receive the gift of assurance, the King will help you know that He loves you, cherishes you, and that you are special to Him and have talents He wants to help you develop. You can know that you are not alone. He will not abandon you or turn His back on you.

The King can replace your darkest fears with the power of His love. He can heal your fear of failure and the disappointments of the past. He accepts you and has awesome plans for you today and each day. You can live with the gift of assurance of His love for you.

2. The Gift of Honesty
The first gift of assurance makes this second gift possible. Without the assurance of acceptance, you will not be able to accept the gift of honesty. You receive this gift by allowing, even inviting the King to help you understand more about yourself. To be honest about

your real motives and deepest fears that push, motivate, drive and inspire you.

The King will help you see some things about yourself that need improvement. At times, He will help you understand hidden feelings and dark desires that you need help in acknowledging to overcome. We can fail to understand how these desires influence our choices. With His help, your fears will not have control over you. Your disappointments can fade in the history of your life. Your challenges don't seem so impossible and you know you have someone, the King, to whom you can talk and be completely honest.

It is interesting to note that if we do not receive the gift of seeing our stealthy self-centeredness, then we will be limited in our understanding of the King. The King seeks to help us understand the difference between the way we think and the way He thinks, and why His way is better. Without understanding why His way is better, we will find ways to justify and rationalize our self-centered desires that lead to bad choices. Then, we would be ignoring the King as He attempts to help us with the gift of being honest.

3. The Gift of Enlightenment
This gift will provide you with hours of joy in your life. This joy comes from learning more *about* the King *from* the King. As you abide in your part of the agreement, He will do whatever it takes to help you understand the difference between His loving way of thinking and your natural, normal human self-first way of thinking. Not in a condemning, you-are-worthless-how-could-you-be-so-stupid way but by reasoning with you as you read His Word.

You can learn about the King from the King, as you read His Word. As you ask for His help, He will help you understand His Word. The King has preserved His Word for us so it can be a light in our lives by helping us understand more about His love and character. His Word is also full of promises that you can claim as your own; promises of peace, wisdom, hope, joy, and the healing of forgiveness.

The King will help you understand His way of thinking presented in His Word and will provide you with the strength to choose and follow through with His way of thinking in choices you face. What a great bargain He provides, a good deal! The King provides all the help you need to enjoy the good life He has for you.

When you read the King's Word, be sure to ask four questions about a story or passage you read. First, how is human selfishness working in this passage? Second, how is the King's love present in the passage? Third, what is the conflict in the passage between human self-centeredness and the King's love? Fourth, what is the solution or lesson to be learned regarding the conflict between human selfishness and the King's love?

4. The Gift of Empowerment to Apologize

Would you rather live knowing about the mistakes you make, the choices that do not reflect the King's way of doing things, or would you like to be in the dark, living apart from the King, yet unaware? We must embrace the reality that selfishness does not create unselfishness. We cannot understand the love behind His unselfish way of thinking without His help.

The gift of being able to apologize flows out of the gifts of assurance, honesty, and being enlightened. Before we can understand that we made a mistake, we must accept the conviction from the King regarding our mistake. To have that kind of a personal relationship with the King that welcomes His advice, correction and council means we know He always has our best interest in mind. The King is always for us and not against us, He has an awesome plan for our lives, and welcoming His input regarding our choices is part of that plan.

The forgiveness the King offers us does not compare to the forgiveness we receive from people. The forgiveness the King offers us will release our guilt, bring peace to our emotions and deep healing to our souls. The same power the King uses to convict us of our mistakes He will use to heal us.

Remember, when you fail to accept His way of thinking as better, and don't let His wisdom and strength provide you with real help in a choice you make, He does not reject you. As you accept His strength to admit your mistake, the King will help you learn from your mistake. He offers you the healing of forgiveness to ease the pain of trying to live without His help.

The King will help you face habits, temptations, and emotional injuries from unfair treatment or anything else that might hinder the awesome plan He has for your life. His forgiveness can heal the deep pain you carry around from past mistakes. His healing renews and empowers your desires, which in turn will lead to choices that honor Him.

5.   The Gift of Discernment to Unmask the Deceptions of the Enemy

You are a child of the King. You have an inheritance. However, you face a villain, an intruder that seeks to make sure that you do not receive your inheritance. He spends His time creating masterful deceptions with lies and half-truths to confuse you. He can present Himself as merciful, seeking to benefit you when he is full of deception and wants to harm you. He seeks to keep you from asking for your inheritance by convincing you that you do not have a problem that the King needs to help you solve.

With the gift of discernment, the King will help you understand the difference between reality and fiction. He will enable you to experience a fresh, vibrant, and healing relationship in which you understand and embrace the power of His love each day.

The King can give you clarity to avoid the deceptions of the villain.

As we have seen, there are five gifts that help us move AHEAD with the King's plan. The five gifts in our inheritance create the acronym AHEAD (Assurance, Honest, Enlighten, Apologize, and Discernment). These five gifts enable us to keep moving forward with the King and His plan for our lives. We receive these gifts by grace through faith as we ask for the King's help to trust in Him.

Remember, faith is not just trusting in the King; faith means you ask for His *help* to trust in Him. He answers your request for help with the five gifts in your inheritance. Then you can enjoy a real, personal relationship with the King where He provides you with real help as you face challenges, trials, issues, and temptations. He can help you with the self-focus problem all humans have and empower you to overcome the villain. You can experience the power of His love, joy, peace, patience, kindness, goodness, gentleness, faithfulness and self-control in your heart each day.

Part Five

Beware of the Villain Who Seeks to Steal Your Inheritance

There is a villain, a con artist, with years of experience, who seeks to swindle us out of our inheritance and, thus, deny us the opportunity to live the awesome plan the King has for our lives. The villain understands how humans think. He studies our weaknesses so he can use them against us. He's a skilled con artist and will use lies, deception, half-truths, and distortions to deceive us.

The villain enjoys leading people to inaccurate perceptions of the King's character. He seeks to make the King look ineffective because of the disasters, abuse, starvation, prejudice, wars, hate crimes and inequalities that exist. So people think, if the King is all-powerful why do we have so many serious problems in the world today? The villain seeks to accuse the King of the injustices that he is responsible for creating.

The villain is a con artist who seeks to bamboozle you. You are the mark and He has a deception for you, to swindle you. How can the villain swindle, bamboozle, con and cheat people? There are three basic ways he swindles people who do not believe in the King and three ways he cons people who do believe in the King.

With people who do not believe, he likes to swindle some with false information about the natural world. He leads them to accept the Theory of Evolution as a fact, so they fail to recognize that they are a child of the King, designed and created by Him. Then the villain persuades them to stand up and defend the lies he has created, thus cutting them off from listening to solid scientific discoveries that reveal Creation. They often conclude that only simple-minded people reject the Theory of Evolution.

The villain also enjoys leading some people to think that with so many different religions, teaching so many different things, who can be correct? Therefore, these people do not seek a relationship with the King because of all the contrary religious teachings in our world today.

The villain has another way of discrediting the King and deceiving people. He encourages people to think that they do not need a Savior, that the King's death on the cross did not accomplish anything. They choose to live without a Savior, a Messiah, a King of Kings who died to take the penalty of sin for those who follow Him.

It is amazing to realize that since faith is asking the King for help to trust in Him, if someone wondered about needing a Savior to die on the cross for him or her, all they would need to do is ask the King. A simple prayer something like this: *I do not know about Christianity, and some Christians do not act very nice. Is Christianity real? Do I need a Savior to die on the cross for me?* This represents a prayer of faith that the King will not ignore and He will answer by providing opportunities to understand more about the cross.

The villain does not just deceive people into rejecting the King; he also has ways to scam or con believers too. He enjoys convincing some people that they can call themselves Christian, and yet not take time to pray, or learn more about the King in His Word, or fellowship and worship with other followers each week. They consider themselves believers, yet they have been conned. They are victims of the villain. He has stolen the joy that comes from prayer, reading the Word, worship, and fellowship.

The villain also likes to attack believers in their most vulnerable spot, the way humans naturally think. In this way, he can keep some Christians from asking for the King's help to trust in Him. The gifts the King provides in our inheritance challenge the self-centered way humans naturally think, and that makes some Christians uncomfortable. Therefore, they don't embrace the gifts in their inheritance. So, instead of enjoying a real relationship with the King, they enjoy church politics and manipulating situations to suit their perspective. Gossip, being critical of others, and telling half-truths become the acceptable norm. They find value in being political troublemakers instead of team players. Unfortunately, this group of people has made many churches ineffective.

The villain will try another way to defraud Christians. He leads them to become uncertain or confused about what they believe so they discount the importance of what they believe. They come to think that what they believe about the King is not as important as just believing the King exists.

The swindler, the villain who cons people out of their inheritance, uses the same basic con with all these situations, with both believers and unbelievers. His goal is the same for all he seeks to swindle. He knows that if he can keep people from living a life of faith, to keep them from asking for the King's help, and thus keep them from receiving the gifts in their inheritance, then he can deceive them.

Part Six

Help from the King's Word

If we try to have a relationship with the King without embracing the agreement He designed, we will eventually come to a place where we resist His love, yet see ourselves as religious. Then as we continue to neglect the real help He offers us, resentment toward the King and His way of thinking can take root in our hearts.

When a religious leader named Nicodemus sought an interview with the King of Kings, he showed his resentment. After telling Nicodemus that he needed to be born again, Nicodemus responded, "How can a man be born again when he is old? Can he enter a second time into his mother's womb and be born?" (John 3:4 NKJ) If we ignore or deny the difference in how we think and the way the King thinks, not only can resentment of His love grow in our hearts but we can become blind to the fact that we resent His love. That is not good.

To help us understand why we need to ask for the King's help and to provide examples of how the five gifts in our inheritance (Assurance, Honesty, Enlightenment, Apology, Discernment) work, the King provides us with His Word, the Bible. His Word enables us to understand the King's character, to get to know Him, to understand His way of thinking and why it's better than our way of thinking. His Word explains the agreement He designed for us, how it works and why we need the agreement.

The Word of the King is not like any other book we read. By being our personal tutor as we read, the King helps us understand His Word. And it's not in a way that we can understand scientifically or test in a lab. As we read, He will *open our understanding* about His way of thinking.

We need help to understand His Word because there are not any books today written in the same style. For example, you can read a passage of ten verses in the New Testament and find ten different topics in the passage. With His Word, we need to put the pieces together as we read. We need to read with faith, asking for His help to understand. Therefore, we must read His Word slowly, thoughtfully, prayerfully, asking for the King's help because His Word is not a finished book. We finish or put the pieces together as the King helps us compare and connect different passages in their proper context. In other words, the *Bible explains and defines itself.*

The King's Word also presents topics as a sculpture instead of a one dimensional, flat painting. For example, if we look at the plan of salvation as a topic in His Word, the front of the "salvation sculpture" can represent the power of the King's grace, His unmerited favor for us as a loving parent favors their child. If we go to the back of the "salvation sculpture," it represents accountability for our choices. There is a judgment and the King will hold us responsible for our choices.

So, how can the topic of salvation teach us that the King offers us all-powerful grace that means we can't earn our salvation by what we do, yet then also hold us accountable for what we do? Here's how it works: in the "salvation sculpture", when you stand beside the sculpture, between the grace in front and the judgment in back, you will see the agreement. As we ask for help from the King and even ask for His help to *ask* for help, He will provide the five gifts in our inheritance to empower a personal relationship with Him. Our personal relationship with Him provides us with the healing of forgiveness for our mistakes and the strength to follow His awesome plan for our lives.

His plan for our lives includes understanding the unknown: the difference between the King's way of thinking and our way of thinking. His Word helps us get to know the real King and the way He thinks. It awakens us to understand that He is loving, kind, forgiving, victorious, healing, all-powerful, and wonderful! His Word reveals the King as the provider of wisdom and courage and that He is compassionate, reproving, committed, and accepting! His Word reveals the King is both Creator and Savior.

In your relationship with the King, how you picture Him, what you believe about His character, will influence your relationship with Him. Do you think of the King as a taskmaster or more like a Santa Claus figure? Do you know the King based upon the help He has given you to understand His Word or have your disappointments and what you have been told about the King shaped your opinion? If you have a view of the King's character that's not based upon the King's Word, it can be difficult to get to know Him as the kind, loving, and abundant provider of unmerited favor. And that's completely understandable.

In a conversation the King had with a woman beside a well, He illustrated the importance of an honest, open, soul-searching relationship with Him that His Word can help us to experience. The following represents a paraphrased, present tense account of the King's encounter with that woman, as taken from John's Gospel, chapter four. Jesus sits at a well in Samaria waiting for His disciples to return from a run to town to get food. Sitting alone, He takes time to think about recent events. Disappointment fills His heart as He thinks about how some of the religious leaders intentionally create division between His disciples and the disciples of John the Baptist. Then the sound of footsteps interrupts His solitude. Making a visor with His hand to shield his eyes from the sun, he spots a woman approaching. She is alone and carries an empty water pot. The woman, catching a glimpse of a man she does not know and who is dressed in the fashion of the Jews, keeps her eyes down, not wanting to engage in conversation. The Jews usually treated the Samaritans as second-class people.

The woman has come to the well for one purpose— water. She made the journey during the hottest part of the day to avoid the crowds of women who come to the well during the cooler hours of the morning. She seeks to avoid the women who enjoy a bit of gossip and ridicule concerning the choices she has made in life. As she fills her water pot, Jesus and the woman remain silent. Then as she turns to make her escape, Jesus breaks the silence.

"Will you give me a drink?"[1] He says. The woman stops, looks at Jesus and reveals her surprise. "You are a Jew and I am a Samaritan woman. How can you ask me for a drink?"[2] The comment does not stick as Jesus deflects her words by saying, "If you knew the gift of God and who it is that asks you for a drink, you would have asked him and he would have given you living water."[3] Stating the obvious, she observes, "you have nothing to draw with and the well is deep. Where can you get this living water?"[4]

Looking down at the well, Jesus speaks again. "Everyone who drinks this water will be thirsty again, but whoever drinks the water

---

1 John 4:7
2 John 4:9
3 John 4:10
4 John 4:11

I give him will never thirst. Indeed, the water I give him will become in him a spring of water welling up to eternal life."[5]

The woman tightens her eyebrows and, with a hint of curiosity in the tone of her voice, retorts, "Sir, give me this water so that I won't get thirsty and have to keep coming here to draw water."[6] With deep, penetrating eyes, Jesus looks at her and says , "Go, call your husband and come back."[7] The blank expression on her face exposes how an unseen force just struck hard at her heart and left her dumbfounded. Fighting back the flood of emotions and hoping to ward off further inquiry, she says in a soft voice, "I have no husband."[8]

Jesus commends her honesty and reveals what else He knows. "The fact is, you have had five husbands, and the man you now have is not your husband. What you have just said is quite true."[9] Like an unfaithful husband standing before his wife holding a hotel room receipt she found in the trash, or a teenager looking at his mother holding the bag of dope she found in his sock drawer, the truth about the woman at the well just got exposed.

Reacting to the forcefulness of His honesty and, in an effort to redirect the flow of conversation, she turns to a contemporary controversy between the Jews and the Samaritans. Yet, Jesus refuses to become defensive.

The conversation has not been going as the woman expected. In fact, a strange excitement has been building in her heart, soothing her deep pain. She has felt acceptance, love and compassion, even though Jesus knows all about her past, her unhealthy choices,

---

5 John 4:13,14
6 John 4:15
7 John 4:16
8 John 4:17
9 John 4:18

and her ugly mistakes. With a sparkle of hope in her eyes, she says, "I know that Messiah is coming. When He comes, He will tell us all things."

Jesus looks into her eyes, the windows of her soul, and says, "I who speak to you am He."[10] Just then, the disciples break into the scene, surprise marking their faces as they see their Master talking with a Samaritan woman. Their arrival halts her dialogue with her Creator before she can respond to His last comment. What does the woman do next? She leaves her water pot at the well and hurries into the city to tell others about the Man she has met.

The woman at the well found freedom, not condemnation, in her honest talk with the King. The same woman who avoided others by coming to the well at noon approaches people in town, proclaiming the message, "Come, see a Man who told me all things that I ever did."[11]

Now, just for clarity, did Jesus really tell her in that short conversation all the things that she ever did? No, obviously not. Yet, she was convinced that He could have done so and that what He did say summed up the truth about her life.

Why did this woman get so excited about an encounter with a man who told her all things she ever did? Would such an encounter excite you if it meant the full exposure of all the things that you ever did? Do we really want everyone—or, even anyone—to know *all* things we have done? I think as far as most people are concerned, the skeletons can just stay in the closet.

How did the people of the town respond after they heard from the Man who knows all? They told the woman, "We no longer believe just because of what you said; now we have heard for ourselves, and

---

10 John 4:26
11 John 4:29

we know that this man really is the Savior of the world."[12] They now grasped a great truth: the successful life the King has for us can unfold as we are willing to be honest with Him about our need for His help.

It's vital for us to ask for the King's help as we read His Word because He wants to reason with us. How can He reason with us and help us understand the difference between the way we think and the way He thinks if we don't invite Him to help us realize the truth about ourselves? In the same way the King helped the woman at the well, He seeks to help us understand more about ourselves and about Him as we read His Word.

The King's Word helps us understand His character, to get to know Him and to embrace His plan for our lives. As we read His Word we need to do so with faith in our hearts, meaning that we need to ask for His help to understand and apply His Word. If we ask, He will teach us how to ask for and receive His help.

His Word provides us with examples and explanations about how to live by asking for help, and how to accept the gifts in our inheritance. His Word helps us know that He loves us, accepts us, that we can have the assurance of His devotion to us. We can read examples of people who discovered that being honest with the King about the desires deep in their hearts brought freedom. We can embrace His power to help us apologize to Him and to others for our mistakes.

We can receive the discernment to unmask the deceptions of the villain, the deceptions that make the King's word confusing or the deceptions about ourselves such as not being smart, pretty, useful, talented, capable, successful or valuable.

You are a child of the King with a problem and an inheritance that can solve your problem. Your inheritance will enable you to

---

12   John 4:42

know the unknown. To know in what ways you need to ask for and receive His help so you can understand why His way of thinking is best. The King's Word will help you understand how the five gifts in your inheritance reveal your human selfishness and the power of the King's unfailing love. Then, you can receive more of His help with the challenges, situations, and issues you face in life.

Part Seven

Knowing the Unknown

With the King's help you can have an honest, non-fluff, non-sugarcoated relationship with the King who can provide you with real help for the situations and challenges you face. You can live an awesome life as you ask for the King's help, which means you are open to a life where you trust in him with the unknown. Living with this perspective means that you do not have to settle for mild, mundane, routine prayers like the "Thank You for our milk and bread, workers kind and good. Amen." Don't settle for prayers that put formula over a relationship, routine over honesty, or denial over positive change.

What might a "please help me to understand in what ways I need your help" prayer sound like? For example, imagine if someone you knew had a problem with anger. They've been praying about the problem for over ten years with little or no improvement. Then you share with them about the agreement and they start asking for Jesus' help to receive the five gifts in their inheritance. With the gifts working in their heart, they begin to pray like this: "My King, I ask for Your help to know in what ways I need to ask for your help regarding my anger." Within weeks the King helps them understand that they use their anger to manipulate people. So now, they understand why just praying about anger did not address the real issue.

As they begin to ask the King for help to stop manipulating people, they start getting the victory over their anger problem as they pray like this: "My King, thank You for showing me how I manipulate people. That was unknown to me. You have helped me understand how I use my anger to get my way. I also use it to defend myself so that I don't have to deal with my real issues. The truth is, You have revealed to me that I like my anger, it feels comfortable and I use it to get what I want. I understand that You have a better way for me to respond than to get angry. I need Your help to know why I enjoy manipulating people. I praise You, for You are loving, kind, patient and all powerful. You accept me and have an awesome plan for my life. You taught that anger will lead to murder and anger is the spirit of murder. I need Your help. Thank you for Your forgiveness for my controlling, manipulative ways." The King helped this person understand how what was unknown controlled their life in a negative way.

If someone is having difficulty finding a job, what might a faithful (asking for the King's help) prayer sound like? "My King, I am disappointed and frustrated about not finding a job. I feel so helpless, nothing is working out for me. I interview for a job yet am not hired. I have put in so many resumes that I do not even remember all the places I have sent them. Please help me know in what ways I need to ask for Your help." Do you think the King can bring real help to this person?

If you are thinking about getting married, what might a faithful (asking for help) prayer sound like? "My King, my Lord, as you know, I am thinking about getting married. Getting married scares me. I believe I am in love, but will that change over the years? I know I have received Your help as I have asked if this is a good match for me. Please, I need Your help to know in what ways I need to ask for Your help as I consider getting married."

If someone has a problem with pornography, what kind of help might the King be able to provide as they pray this prayer: "I acknowledge to You, my King, that when I walk by the huge, bigger than life posters at Victoria's Secret in the mall I can't stop thinking about those images. So, when I get home, I get online and click on sites that I know do not honor You. I find myself looking at things that I know You do not want me to see. You have helped me understand that there is a part of me that enjoys looking at those websites, that I enjoy the fantasy relationships with these women because then I do not have to deal with the challenges of a real relationship. I know these desires in my heart do not honor You. You taught that the kind of lust I have in my heart is not healthy and will lead me away from Your plan for my life. I ask for Your forgiveness. I ask for the healing You promise to provide. Thank you for helping me understand the desires in my heart that drive me to see women as a toy to play with instead of a person to respect."

When we engage our King by asking for His help to trust in Him, He will answer us with the real help the five gifts in our inheritance provide. Then we can have a personal relationship with the King where He can help us understand more about His plan with the situations and challenges we face. In fact, did you know that each day our King asks us, "What do you want Me to do for you?"

In the King's Word, there is a story about a man called blind Bartimaeus that reveals the King's desire to help us. One day, Jesus came near, and blind Bartimaeus called out saying, "Jesus, Son of David, have mercy on me."[13] Jesus stopped and asked him, "What do you want me to do for you?"[14] What a great response. The King

---

13 Mark 10:47
14 Mark 10:51

of Kings was ready to help at his request. Blind Bartimaeus then said, "Rabbi, I want to see." [15] Jesus responded, "Go your way; your faith has healed you."[16]

Do you realize that just like the King was eager and ready to help blind Bartimaeus, He is ready to help you? In fact, every morning the King asks you, "What do you want Me to do for you today?" You can ignore Him and miss what He wants to do for you, or you can live by faith as you ask for His help to receive the gifts in your inheritance each day.

As you receive the gifts in your inheritance, the King can help you know more about unknown consequences from your choices. Just think, if you knew about negative consequences that could follow a choice you made, would you make that choice? The King will help you understand the consequences of self-centered choices before you decide what to do. It is not a guarantee that you won't ever suffer bad consequences from your choices, yet He can help you understand why His way is better.

As you receive the gifts in your inheritance, the King can help you with unknown desires in your heart that influence you. Deep in your heart, you can be unaware of how negative experiences have entrenched self-centered desires into your thinking. You can be blind to how past issues impact your choices. The King can help you know if you have any unresolved anger, frustration, discouragement, irritations, or disappointments that influence your choices today. We all have unresolved issues that continue to influence us in unknown ways. Our compassionate King, with gentle kindness, will help you know the unknown issues in your heart that can be a problem. As you receive the gifts in your inheritance, the King can help you with

---

15 Ibid
16 Mark 10:52

unknown options. You can be blind to His positive options for the choices you face if you fail to ask for His help. In all the choices you make each day, you can ask for the King's help to know how His way of thinking provides positive options. He is always ready to help you know your next step with the issues you face. As you receive the gifts in your inheritance, the King can help you with unknown outcomes that surprise you. When you are confronted with a challenge, your first response does not need to be fear. With any challenge you face, the King can help you trust in Him with unknown outcomes from that challenge. Like not knowing how you can pay the bills after being laid off from work, or trying to figure out how to pay for an unexpected, expensive car repair. The gifts in your inheritance lead you to a relationship with the King that will help you trust in Him with unknown outcomes from the challenges you face. As you ask for the King's help to trust in Him, asking Him to help you know in what ways you need His help, He provides the five gifts (AHEAD) in your inheritance. Then you can enjoy the freedom of a real, personal relationship with Him each day. He can help you with unknown outcomes, unknown consequences, unknown desires and to become aware of unknown options.

ELIJAH AND THE WIDOW

In the story of Elijah and the widow of Zarephath, God led Elijah to challenge a poor widow to trust in God with the unknown. In this classic Old Testament story, I can imagine the widow hunched down near the city gate, picking up a few sticks for a fire. A man approaches, catching her attention. She looks up as he comes closer and utters a request, "Would you bring me a little water in a jar so I may have a drink?"[17] She straightens out her weak legs to fetch

---

17   1 Kings 17:10

the water. But, as she turns to go, the man adds, "And bring me, please, a piece of bread."[18] I can imagine how, upon hearing his request, her eyebrows push down and her mouth pops open as she responds in a solemn yet frustrated tone, "I was just out here gathering sticks for a small fire, so that I can take my last handful of flour and the last few drops of oil I have to bake a small cake of bread for my son and myself before we starve to death." We could call this moment her tipping point. She is willing to get the prophet some water, but giving him their last morsel of food is too much. Her response shows her loss of hope. Yet Elijah won't back down and challenges her. "Don't be afraid...first make a small cake of bread for me from what you have and bring it to me, and then make something for yourself and your son."[19]

Oddly, Elijah did not offer her consolation. No soft, compassionate words dropped from his lips. He didn't say, "Oh, that's OK, I know it's been hard. Forget what I said. You don't have to get me any food." Instead, he challenged her. He pressed her on the point. How could Elijah do this? The woman must have thought, *You don't get it, do you? I have only enough flour for one small cake. How can you ask me for our last meal?* Yet, Elijah gave her a promise to trust in. "For this is what the LORD, the God of Israel, says: 'The jar of flour will not be used up and the jug of oil will not run dry until the day the LORD gives rain on the land.'"[20]

God created a struggle with the unknown for this widow: eat the last bit of food and die, or give it to Elijah and trust in God with the unknown. When she mixed the flour in a bowl and waited for the bread to bake, did she perhaps review her options? Did she think: *This drought has been awful; should I trust what Elijah has said?*

---

18 1 Kings 17:11
19 1 Kings 17:13
20 1 Kings 17:14

Does it really matter? We will all be dead soon anyway. Yet, might Elijah's promise be true? In the end, she decided to trust in God with the unknown, to give her last bit of food to Elijah. It was at this point that the promise of God became a reality—a reality that lasted until the end of the drought. Each day God provided her with enough flour and oil—but just enough for a single day. Just imagine how she felt as she emptied the flour bin and oil jar each day, then came back the next day to find enough flour and oil for another day. In the same way, the King can challenge us to trust in Him with unknown issues we face. The widow felt abandoned, left to die, and beyond help. Yet, she chose to reject a pessimistic perspective and accepted the words Elijah spoke to her about the flour and oil not running dry. We can have the same challenge with the unknown as the widow. We do not think as the King thinks, and at times He will challenge us to trust in Him. Yet, just as with the widow, the King provides what we need to trust in Him.

Part Eight

The King's Awesome Plan for Your Life

The King provides an inheritance (AHEAD), by grace (free) through faith (we ask for help to trust in Him) that will empower us to have a real, personal relationship with Him that provides help with the issues and challenges we face. He can teach us how to trust in Him with the unknown. He will also help us know what is real in His Word and give us the strength to act on what we believe.

As the gifts in our inheritance work in our hearts, we can know in what ways we need to ask for His help. Then the King can help us live the awesome plan He has for our lives. He will help our character to develop, so we make more choices based on His love, joy, peace, patience, kindness, goodness, gentleness, faithfulness, self-control and forgiveness in our hearts.

As you continue to ask for the King's help, the five gifts in your inheritance will empower a relationship with the King that you will want to share with other people. He can provide opportunities for you to help people in the community to get to know Him. You might encounter people who have been searching for answers and you get to share with them about the inheritance the King provides. You also might be inspired to show the King's love in practical ways to people in the community. For example, if you can paint, rake leaves, pick up trash, fix cars, make paper airplanes, fix dinner, hammer a nail, create flower arrangements, make cards, run, ride a bike, work out with weights, play the piano, make wooden toys, play golf, create computer programs, or whatever, you can ask (faith) and the King will help you find ways to connect with other people through the talents and abilities He has given you.

As the King opens opportunities for you to connect with others, through the process of time, you will have opportunities to share with them about how the King has helped you. Just imagine the wonderful feeling of accomplishment as you help others discover the joy of receiving their inheritance and receiving real help from the King.

The King will not only lead you to help others outside the church, He will empower you to help people in the church. You may like to teach Bible lessons to adults, teens or children, help with fellowship meals, welcome people at the door, help with socials or fun events, teach life skills or many other ways that the King can empower you to encourage and help members.

REAL HELP THAT PROVIDES A NEW PERSPECTIVE

The King gives us a new perspective each day, one based on His love instead of our self-centeredness. The King told a story that illustrates the amazing power He has to change our perspective. It is a story about some workers on a farm. In retelling this story found in Matthew 20:1-16 as a paraphrase, I would like to give the landowner a name: Jesse.

Here's what happened in the story. It was harvest time and Jesse needed some workers for his farm. He went to town early, at 6:00 in the morning to hire some local workers. They agreed to work for $150 for the day. Other farm owners might cheat their workers, if they could, and pay them only a half-day's wages for a full day's work, but not Jesse.

As the day continued, Jesse kept looking for more people to work on his farm. At 9:00 in the morning, he went back to town to hire more workers, then again at noon, and again at 3:00 in the afternoon. To each new group he told them, "You also go to work on my farm and I will pay you what is right."

Finally, at 5:00 in the afternoon, just one hour before quitting time, he went back to town and found a few more workers who had not yet been hired. He told them, "Go work on my farm, and I will pay you what is right."

At six o'clock in the evening, quitting time, he instructed his foreman to line up all the workers to receive their pay, with the last ones hired being first in line. As Jesse began to pay the workers, the first ones hired, who had been working all day, got excited. They saw Jesse give $150 to those who worked for only a single hour. They all smiled at each other. They thought that certainly they would get more than the agreed amount. It would only be fair. They had worked all day in the hot sun. Logic and equity dictate that they should receive more than those who only worked for a single hour.

As they stood in line, I can imagine their conversation. "Maybe we'll get a $150 for every hour that we've worked today. Then we won't have to work for several weeks!" However, when Jesse put $150 in their hands, they cry out, "That's not fair! Everyone has received the same pay, no matter how long or hard they worked."

Jesse responded, "I have done you no wrong. This is my farm, and this is my money; I can do with it as I please. You agreed to work all day for $150. I have done what I said I would do." The workers who labored all day expected more. But wouldn't you? It's just common sense that if you work more you should get paid more.

40

In this story, there's a dilemma created between what could be considered fair (the amount of pay given to the workers who did not work all day) and what the landowner could do with his own money. Yet, because the workers who agreed to work for a full day's pay called into question the generous landowner's fairness, they revealed an attitude that the King could not endorse. Jesse told them, "Don't I have the right to do what I want with my own money? Or are you envious because I am generous?"[21]

This story highlights what happens when we ask for and receive our inheritance: the King will provide a radical new way of thinking. Just imagine if the workers who labored all day had a different perspective, a radical perspective. What if after they received the same pay as those who only worked for one hour, they rejoiced? Instead of being offended, they would say, "Yes, this landowner is awesome, he is so generous. I can't believe he was willing to give so much to those who only worked for one hour. When I saw the look of surprise upon those who worked for only one hour but received a full day's pay I wanted to cry. They thought they had been overlooked and forgotten. They had been in town ready for work and no one showed up until one hour before quitting time. I would love to see the look on the faces of their families when they find out that they got $150 for one hour. This is the kind of person I want to work for, and I want to come back tomorrow and work all day again. I can't wait to see the surprised look on the faces of the people who work for one hour and get paid for a full day." When the King gives you the inheritance He desires to provide, the freedom and joy you discover will give you a radical, new, loving perspective.

You were born a child of the King, and He has an inheritance for you. You could never earn what He seeks to give you. Your

---

21 Matthew 20:15

inheritance includes the gift of assurance, the gift of being honest about the desires in your heart, the gift of being enlightened about His way of thinking and why it is best, the gift of apology, and the gift of discernment to unmask the deceptions of the thieving villain. All these gifts work together to enable you to ask for the King's help to know the ways you need to ask for His help.

You can receive the gifts in your inheritance as you accept the fact that you have a problem that needs to be solved. Then you can take the next step of living by faith. In other words, when you take the first step of accepting that you need a Savior, your part of the agreement is to live by faith. Living by faith means asking for His help to trust in Him, you know you need help from your Savior. Then He can then provide you with the gifts that empower a real, personal relationship with the King that yields fruit from the power of His love each day. You can know what is real in His Word and enjoy the power of His love, joy, peace, patience, kindness, goodness, gentleness, faithfulness, self-control and forgiveness each day.

Our problem is not just a behavior challenge with obedience being the solution. The tug of war between our selfish desires and Jesus' love presents a more complex challenge. If our behavior were the whole problem, the solution would be simple: spiritual boot camp. We could focus on books and classes that train us how to have a strong, determined will that just says no. Convinced of the truth, we would obey, and that would be that. Yet it is not that simple. Or should I say, it's not that hard? If we misunderstand the problem, we will not embrace the solution.

We can get the wrong idea about the challenges we face from our innate selfishness. We can think that we have to choose between two earthly things, such as getting angry or not getting angry, stealing or not stealing, doing drugs or not doing drugs, committing adultery or not committing adultery. However, the real choice is whether we ask for His help. Therefore, it's not a choice between getting angry or not, stealing or not, having an affair or not. It is a choice between asking for the King's help or not.

When we ask for His help to trust in Him, He will provide the gifts in our inheritance that help us to get to know ourselves and the King better. Then we can receive real help with our challenges, questions, disappointments, issues and situations we face. We will also enjoy the power of His love, joy, peace, patience, kindness, goodness, gentleness, faithfulness, self-control and forgiveness He gives us each day.

TAKE THE SEVEN-DAY CHALLENGE

Try it for yourself. Read through and pray with one of the outlines in the appendix for seven consecutive days. You may use the following model prayer as a guide to ask for the King's help and receive your inheritance each day.

Dear Jesus, I am Your child and You have an inheritance for me. I would like to respond to the power of Your love that has been working in my life. I believe that I need a Savior to solve my selfishness problem and help me overcome the villain. Thank you for the agreement you designed which allows me to receive the gifts in my inheritance. I acknowledge that Your part of the agreement is to provide what I need by grace. My part of the agreement requires faith. So, I want to ask for your help to trust in You. I believe that I am a sinner, born with a selfishness problem that requires a Savior to solve. I can't understand Your loving way of thinking without Your help. As You provide the gifts in my inheritance, You will enable me to learn how to trust in Your way of thinking and provide the power of Your love, joy, peace, patience, kindness, goodness, gentleness, faithfulness, self-control and forgiveness I need each day. Please help me to receive my inheritance that can solve my selfishness problem, empower me to overcome the villain and live the awesome plan You have for my life.

As a child of the King, you can ask for your inheritance that will empower you with the gifts you need to have a personal relationship with the King. To live a life guided by His wisdom and courage, to receive the healing of forgiveness and the joy that goes with it, and to have His help to understand the unknown. In other words, when you fulfill your part of the agreement by asking for the King's help to trust in Him, you can have a real relationship with the King.

Appendix

1. HOW THE AGREEMENT WORKS IN YOUR LIFE

1. You are a child of the King, born a child of the King, yet with a problem to solve and a villain to overcome.

2. The King has an inheritance for you that provides real help to live the awesome plan He has for your life. The inheritance the King seeks to give you can solve your problem and empower you to overcome the villain.

3. Since the King will not force you to accept His help, He designed an agreement that enables you to receive your inheritance when you accept Him as your Savior.

4. The agreement has two parts: your part and the King's part. Your part of the agreement states that you can receive your inheritance by faith. Many people can fall short with their part of the agreement because they don't embrace what the Bible teaches about faith. Faith means that you believe you need a Savior to help you with your selfishness problem, so therefore need to ask for the King's help each day to trust in His way of thinking. Then, the King's part of the agreement means He provides the gifts in your inheritance that enables a real, open and

honest relationship with Him. You could never earn and you do not deserve the gifts in your inheritance. You receive His help by grace.

5. Your inheritance includes fives gifts that empower a real relationship with the King. Ask the King for help to receive the five gifts in your inheritance each day. (Matthew 7:7-11).

    Assurance - Hebrews 13:5,6
    Honesty - Psalm 139:23,24
    Enlightenment - Proverbs 4:5-7 Proverbs 3:5-7
    Apology - 1 John 1:8,9
    Discernment - 2 Co 11:12-15

6. As the gifts in your inheritance work in your heart, you can move AHEAD with the King's plan for your life and have a real relationship with Him. You can know what is real in His Word, and ask for His help to act on what you believe. He can then help you with the choices, issues, questions and situations you face each day.

7. A real relationship with the King provides help with the unknown.

Unknown Consequences from a Bad Choice - If you knew the unfortunate consequences that would follow some choices you make, you might not make that choice. You can enjoy (at the moment) things that the King does not enjoy. He will help you understand the difference between the way He thinks and the way you think, and why His way is better for you. Knowing why His way is better will motivate you to ask for His strength to follow His way. Without understanding why His way is better, how can you follow His way?

Unknown Desires will influence us. Deep in your heart, you can be unaware of how self-centered desires drive some of your choices. You can be blind to how current or past experiences impact your thinking today. The King can help you know if you have any un-resolved anger, frustration, discouragement, irritations, or disap-pointments that impact your choices today. Your compassionate King, with gentle kindness, will help you to know any unknown is-sues in your heart that can motivate you.

Unknown Options - You can be blind to His options without a per-sonal relationship with Him that welcomes the gifts in your inheri-tance. With your inheritance, you can ask for His help with the issues that come up throughout each day. In all the choices that you make each day, you can ask for the King's help to know how His way of thinking applies to the decisions before you. He is always ready to help you know your next step. As you ask, He can help you know in what ways you need to ask for His help.

Unknown Outcomes - You can have times when you face problems that can have a negative impact on you. Unknown sudden car repairs, a health issue, or a problem at work are problems that can create a lot of fear in your life. You can face these problems with real help from the King as you receive the five gifts in your inheritance. Then the King can help you trust in Him with unknown outcomes you face.

8. You face a villain that seeks to make sure that you do not ask for the King's help; that you do not live with a personal relation-ship with the King. With some people, the villain cons them into believing the King does not exist. For others, He swindles them out of their inheritance by leading them to accept false teach-ings about the King. With others, the villain seeks to keep them focused on believing that a relationship with the King is based on rules. This means people become deceived by using rules as a means of salvation or see the impossibility of keeping the

rules and come to believe that obedience is not important. The villain also enjoys tempting and hassling those who seek to live with a personal relationship with the King.

9. You have the Word of the King that informs you about a correct understanding of the character of the King. His Word also helps you understand about receiving the gifts in your inheritance by grace (receiving what you do not deserve) through faith (asking for His help). His Word reveals how He will use these five gifts to help you each day. The King's word will have a new clarity as you realize that faith is asking for His help to trust in Him. He will use His Word to enlighten you about the difference between how He thinks and how you think.

10. As you continue to humbly ask for real help from a real King, asking for His help to accept and understand how the five gifts work in your life, then you can live as a child of the King, enjoying a personal relationship with Him. The King will help you know the unknown: He will help you know in what ways you need to ask for His help. Then He can provide the real help you need. He will empower you to use the talents He has given you to help others in the church and community. He will provide opportunities for you to share with others about how the King has helped you. He will provide continuous access to His love, joy, peace, patience, kindness, goodness, gentleness, faithfulness, self-control and forgiveness to help you move AHEAD with His plan for your life.

2. *OUTLINE WITH BIBLE VERSES*
YOU ARE A CHILD OF THE KING.

You are a child of the King, born as a child of the King. (Genesis 1:26,27; Acts 17:26-31; Ephesians 2:10; Romans 9:17-20; Psalm 53:1,2).

As a child of the King, you may receive an inheritance that will help you experience for yourself the power of His love to its fullest. (2 Peter 1:2-4; Romans 12:2; Psalm 51:10).

However, there is a problem. While you were born a child of the King, you were also born separated from the King. (Matthew 9:11-13; Romans 3:23; Romans 6:23; Mark 7:20-23).

You also face a villain who seeks to keep you from getting any help from the King regarding your problem. (Ephesians 6:11-16; 2 Corinthians 11:12-15).

Therefore, the King designed an agreement that enables you to receive your inheritance. The gifts in your inheritance will solve your problem and enable you to overcome the villain. (Acts 2:38,39; Ephesians 2:8; Philippians 2:13; Titus 3:5; 2 Corinthians 5:17; Ezekiel 36:26; Romans 15:13).

The Agreement has Two Parts
The King's Part - The King has an inheritance He wants to give us by grace. The gifts in our inheritance provide real help each day to understand more about the difference between His way of thinking and our way of thinking. Because all humans have turned away from following the King, we need His help to recover what we have lost.

We do not deserve the gifts He seeks to provide, and we could never earn the right to receive the inheritance He wants to give us. (2 Corinthians 12:9; Hebrews 4:16; James 4:6; Titus 2:11; Romans 6:14).

Our Part - Our part of the agreement is to live by faith. Faith means we believe that we need a Savior, that we must have His help. We believe that we are born with a self-focus and need His help to trust in Him. Sometimes people can have difficulty with asking for the King's help. However, we can ask for His help to ask for His help. Then He can help us understand why we need His help, and it becomes easier to ask for His help. He will not force us. As we ask for His help, He can provide us with the gifts in our inheritance that we need to get to know Him and experience the power of His love. You can try this yourself to see if it is true, by simply asking for His help to receive and understand each of the five gifts in your inheritance each day. As these gifts work upon your heart, He can provide real help with issues, challenges and situations you face. (Proverbs 3:5,6; Matthew 7:7-11).

The Five Gifts in our Inheritance Enable us to Experience the Power of His Love

1. The gift of **A**ssurance. Each morning and evening ask the King to help you understand how much He loves you and that He accepts you and has an awesome plan for your life. (Psalm 23:4; Romans 8:1; Philippians 1:6; 2 Corinthians 4:8-10; 1 John 4:18).
2. The gift of **H**onesty. Ask for His help to be honest about the desires in your heart that do not honor the King. (Psalm 139:23,24; 1 Corinthians 3:18; Psalm 119:36,37; Psalm 26:2; Psalm 19:12).
3. The gift of **E**nlightenment. Ask for His help to understand the difference between His way of thinking and your way of thinking and why His loving way of thinking is better as you read

His Word. Then, as you understand why His way of thinking is better, you can ask for and receive the strength to choose and follow through with His way of thinking. (Psalm 119:105; Psalm 119:130; John 8:32; John 16:13; Psalm 25:5; 2 Timothy 3:16-17).

4. The gift of being able to **A**pologize. Ask for His help to understand when you should apologize to Him and others you have injured. Invite the King to help you own your mistakes and turn them into opportunities to learn more about His way of thinking. You can receive the healing of forgiveness that we all need. (1 John 1:8,9; Colossians 3:13; Matthew 6:14-15; Ephesians 4:31-32; Isaiah 43:25; Ephesians 1:7; Psalm 103:12).

5. The gift of **D**iscernment. Ask for His help to unmask the deceptions of the villain, to not let the villain, the con artist, the liar, the hater, swindle you out of the King's plan for your life. (James 1:5; Colossians 1:13-14; 1 John 3:8; John 8:44; James 4:7; 1 Peter 5:8-9; 1 Corinthians 2:14; 1 Timothy 4:1).

These five gifts form the acronym **AHEAD.** You can move **AHEAD** with the King's plan for your life each day as you experience the power of His love to its fullest. These five gifts will enable you to experience the joy and peace He brings and the healing of forgiveness we all need. Just try it. You can test this for yourself and see that it is true.

Living by faith means asking for the King's help each day to trust in Him each day. Then you can receive your inheritance. The gifts in your inheritance will bless your life in two ways. First, to help you solve the problem that has separated you from the King so you can experience the power of His love for yourself. Second, your inheritance will empower you to overcome the villain's temptations and deceptions. You can know that what you believe about the King is real and true, then you can ask for His help to act on what you believe.

The five gifts in your inheritance all work together to enable you to receive help with challenges and issues you face. Without the five gifts in your inheritance, you won't receive the help you need to trust in Him, experience His love, receive the healing of forgiveness and follow His plan for your life.

3. BIBLE SOLUTIONS: QUESTIONS FOR ANY BIBLE PASSAGE OR STORY

Answering the four questions below will help you become more enlightened to the difference between the way humans think and the way the King thinks as you read His Word. These questions will also help you understand more about grace, faith, the five gifts in your inheritance and the agreement the King designed for you. Just apply these questions to any passage or story you read in the King's Word.

1. How is human selfishness working in the story or passage?
2. How is the King's love present in the passage?
3. What is the conflict in the passage between human self-centeredness and the King's love?
4. What is the solution or lesson to be learned regarding the conflict between human selfishness and the King's love?

Made in the USA
Monee, IL
27 February 2022

91946260R00035